CROCK·POT.
· THE ORIGINAL SLOW COOKER ·

Desserts

D1451649

Publications International, Ltd.

Copyright © 2016 Publications International, Ltd.
Recipes and text on pages 4–5, 7, 12, 16, 18, 24, 28, 34, 44, 50, 54, 61, 62, 68, 71, 82 and 96 © 2016 Sunbeam Products, Inc. doing business as Jarden Consumer Solutions. All rights reserved. All other recipes and all photographs © 2016 Publications International, Ltd.

This publication may not be reproduced or quoted in whole or in part by any means whatsoever without written permission from:

Louis Weber, CEO
Publications International, Ltd.
8140 Lehigh Avenue
Morton Grove, IL 60053

Permission is never granted for commercial purposes.

Crock-Pot® and the Crock-Pot® logo are registered trademarks of Sunbeam Products, Inc. used under license.

Pictured on the front cover *(clockwise from top left):* Mixed Berry Cobbler *(page 62)*, Mexican Chocolate Bread Pudding *(page 12)* and Rocky Road Brownie Bottoms *(page 7)*.

Pictured on the back cover *(left to right):* Bananas Foster *(page 54)*, Easy Chocolate Pudding Cake *(page 14)* and Italian Cheesecake *(page 40)*.

ISBN: 978-1-68022-481-8

Library of Congress Control Number: 2016935638

Manufactured in China.

8 7 6 5 4 3 2 1

Publications International, Ltd.

Table of Contents

Page 61

Slow Cooking Tips

Baked Goods

If you wish to prepare bread, cakes, or pudding cakes in a **CROCK-POT**® slow cooker, you may want to purchase a covered, vented metal cake pan accessory for your **CROCK-POT**® slow cooker. You can also use any straight-sided soufflé dish or deep cake pan that will fit into the stoneware of your unit. Baked goods can be prepared directly in the stoneware; however, they can be a little difficult to remove from the insert, so follow the recipe directions carefully.

Types of CROCK-POT® Slow Cookers

Current **CROCK-POT**® slow cookers come equipped with many different features and benefits, from auto cook programs to oven-safe stoneware to timed programming. Please visit **WWW.CROCK-POT.COM** to find the **CROCK-POT**® slow cooker that best suits your needs.

How you plan to use a **CROCK-POT**® slow cooker may affect the model you choose to purchase. For everyday cooking, choose a size large enough to serve your family. If you plan to use the **CROCK-POT**® slow cooker primarily for entertaining, choose one of the larger sizes. Basic **CROCK-POT**® slow cookers can hold as little as 16 ounces or as much as 7 quarts. The smallest sizes are great for keeping dips warm on a buffet, while the larger sizes can more readily fit large quantities of food and larger roasts.

Sizes of CROCK-POT® Slow Cookers

Smaller **CROCK-POT**® slow cookers—such as 1- to 3½-quart models—are the perfect size for cooking for singles, a couple, or empty nesters (and also for serving dips and fondue).

While medium-size **CROCK-POT**® slow cookers (those holding somewhere between 3 quarts and 5 quarts) will easily cook enough food at one time to feed a small family.

Large **CROCK-POT**® slow cookers are great for large family dinners, holiday entertaining, and potluck suppers. A 6- to 7-quart model is ideal if you like to make meals in advance. Or, have dinner tonight and store leftovers for the next day.

Cooking, Stirring, and Food Safety

CROCK-POT® slow cookers are safe to leave unattended. The outer heating base may get hot as it cooks, but it should not pose a fire hazard. The heating element in the heating base functions at a low wattage and is safe for your countertops.

According to the U.S. Department of Agriculture, all bacteria are killed at a temperature of 165°F. It's important to follow the recommended cooking times and not to open the lid often, especially early in the cooking process when heat is building up inside the unit. If you need to open the lid to check on your food or are adding additional ingredients, remember to allow additional cooking time if necessary to ensure food is cooked through.

Large **CROCK-POT®** slow cookers, the 6- to 7-quart sizes, may benefit from a quick stir halfway through cook time to help distribute heat and promote even cooking. It's usually unnecessary to stir at all, as even ½ cup liquid will help to distribute heat and the stoneware is the perfect medium for holding food at an even temperature throughout the cooking process.

Oven-Safe Stoneware

All **CROCK-POT®** slow cooker removable stoneware inserts may (without their lids) be used safely in ovens at up to 400°F. In addition, all **CROCK-POT®** slow cookers are microwavable without their lids. If you own another slow cooker brand, please refer to your owner's manual for specific stoneware cooking medium tolerances.

Frozen Food

Frozen food can be successfully cooked in a **CROCK-POT®** slow cooker. However, it will require additional cooking time than the same recipe made with fresh food. It is preferable to thaw frozen food prior to placing it in the **CROCK-POT®** slow cooker. Using an instant-read thermometer is recommended to ensure meat is fully cooked through.

Page 40

Chocolate
Lovers

Rocky Road Brownie Bottoms

Makes 6 servings

½ cup packed brown sugar

½ cup water

2 tablespoons unsweetened cocoa powder

2½ cups packaged brownie mix

1 package (about 4 ounces) instant chocolate pudding mix

½ cup milk chocolate chips

2 eggs, beaten

3 tablespoons butter, melted

2 cups mini marshmallows

1 cup chopped pecans or walnuts, toasted*

½ cup chocolate syrup

To toast pecans, spread in single layer in heavy skillet. Cook and stir over medium heat 1 to 2 minutes or until nuts are lightly browned.

1. Coat inside of **CROCK-POT®** slow cooker with nonstick cooking spray. Prepare foil handles by tearing off three 18×2-inch strips heavy foil (or use regular foil folded to double thickness). Crisscross foil strips in spoke design; place in **CROCK-POT®** slow cooker.

2. Combine brown sugar, water and cocoa in small saucepan over medium heat; bring to a boil over medium-high heat.

3. Meanwhile, combine brownie mix, pudding mix, chocolate chips, eggs and butter in medium bowl; stir until well blended. Spread batter in **CROCK-POT®** slow cooker; pour boiling sugar mixture over batter.

4. Cover; cook on HIGH 1½ hours. Turn off heat. Top brownies with marshmallows, pecans and chocolate syrup. Let stand 15 minutes. Use foil handles to lift brownie to serving platter.

Note: Recipe can be doubled for a 5-, 6- or 7-quart **CROCK-POT®** slow cooker.

Hot Fudge Cake

Makes 6 to 8 servings

1½ cups packed light brown sugar, divided

2 cups all-purpose flour

¼ cup plus 3 tablespoons unsweetened cocoa powder, divided, plus additional for dusting

2 teaspoons baking powder

1 teaspoon salt

1 cup milk

¼ cup (½ stick) butter, melted

1 teaspoon vanilla

3½ cups boiling water

1. Coat inside of 5-quart **CROCK-POT**® slow cooker with nonstick cooking spray. Prepare foil handles by tearing off three 18×2-inch strips heavy foil (or use regular foil folded to double thickness). Crisscross foil strips in spoke design; place in **CROCK-POT**® slow cooker.

2. Combine 1 cup brown sugar, flour, 3 tablespoons cocoa, baking powder and salt in medium bowl; stir to blend. Stir in milk, butter and vanilla; stir to blend. Pour into **CROCK-POT**® slow cooker. Combine remaining ½ cup brown sugar and ¼ cup cocoa in small bowl; stir to blend. Sprinkle evenly over mixture in **CROCK-POT**® slow cooker. Pour in boiling water. *Do not stir.*

3. Cover; cook on HIGH 1 to 1½ hours or until toothpick inserted into center comes out clean. Turn off heat. Let stand 10 minutes. Use foil handles to lift cake from **CROCK-POT**® slow cooker onto large serving platter. Cut into wedges to serve. Dust with additional cocoa.

Triple White Chocolate Fantasy

Makes 36 pieces

- 2 pounds white almond bark, broken into pieces
- 1 bar (4 ounces) white chocolate, broken into pieces*
- 1 package (12 ounces) white chocolate chips
- 3 cups candy-coated chocolate pieces or colored sprinkles

*Use your favorite high-quality chocolate candy bar.

1. Place almond bark, chocolate bar and chocolate chips in **CROCK-POT®** slow cooker. Cover; cook on HIGH 1 hour. *Do not stir.*

2. Turn **CROCK-POT®** slow cooker to LOW. Cover; cook on LOW 1 hour, stirring every 15 minutes. Stir in chocolate pieces.

3. Spread mixture onto large baking sheet covered with waxed paper; cool completely. Break into pieces. Store in tightly covered container.

Variations: Here are a few ideas for other imaginative items to add in along with or instead of the candy-coated chocolate pieces: raisins, crushed peppermint candy, crushed toffee, peanuts or pistachio nuts, chopped gum drops, chopped dried fruit or candied cherries.

Mexican Chocolate Bread Pudding

Makes 6 to 8 servings

1½ **cups whipping cream**

4 **ounces unsweetened chocolate, coarsely chopped**

½ **cup currants**

2 **eggs, beaten**

½ **cup sugar**

1 **teaspoon vanilla**

¾ **teaspoon ground cinnamon, plus additional for topping**

½ **teaspoon ground allspice**

⅛ **teaspoon salt**

3 **cups Hawaiian-style sweet bread, challah or rich egg bread, cut into ½-inch cubes**

Whipped cream (optional)

1. Heat cream in large saucepan. Add chocolate; stir until melted.

2. Combine currants, eggs, sugar, vanilla, ¾ teaspoon cinnamon, allspice and salt in medium bowl; stir to blend. Add currant mixture to chocolate mixture; stir to blend. Pour into **CROCK-POT®** slow cooker.

3. Gently fold in bread cubes using plastic spatula. Cover; cook on HIGH 3 to 4 hours or until knife inserted near center comes out clean.

4. Serve warm or chilled. Top with whipped cream sprinkled with additional cinnamon, if desired.

Easy Chocolate Pudding Cake

Makes 16 servings

1 package (6-serving size) instant chocolate pudding and pie filling mix

3 cups milk

1 package (about 18 ounces) chocolate fudge cake mix, plus ingredients to prepare mix

Crushed peppermint candies (optional)

Whipped topping (optional)

1. Coat inside of 4-quart CROCK-POT® slow cooker with nonstick cooking spray. Sprinkle pudding mix into CROCK-POT® slow cooker. Whisk in milk.

2. Prepare cake mix according to package directions. Carefully pour cake mix into CROCK-POT® slow cooker. *Do not stir.* Cover; cook on HIGH 1½ hours or until toothpick inserted into center comes out clean.

3. Spoon into cups; serve warm with crushed peppermint candies and whipped topping, if desired.

Tip: Allow breads, cakes and puddings to cool at least 5 minutes before scooping or removing them from the CROCK-POT® slow cooker.

Bittersweet Chocolate-Espresso Crème Brûlée

Makes 5 servings

- ½ cup chopped bittersweet chocolate
- 5 egg yolks
- 1½ cups whipping cream
- ½ cup granulated sugar
- ¼ cup espresso
- ¼ cup Demerara or raw sugar

1. Arrange five 6-ounce ramekins or custard cups inside of **CROCK-POT®** slow cooker. Pour enough water to come halfway up sides of ramekins (taking care to keep water out of ramekins). Divide chocolate among ramekins.

2. Whisk egg yolks in small bowl; set aside. Heat small saucepan over medium heat. Add cream, granulated sugar and espresso; cook and stir until mixture begins to boil. Pour hot cream in thin, steady stream into egg yolks, whisking constantly. Pour through fine mesh strainer into clean bowl.

3. Ladle into prepared ramekins over chocolate. Cover; cook on HIGH 1 to 2 hours or until custard is set around edges but still soft in centers. Carefully remove ramekins; cool to room temperature. Cover; refrigerate until serving. Spread tops of custards with Demerara sugar just before serving.

Rum and Cherry Cola Fudge Spoon Cake

Makes 8 to 10 servings

½ cup cola
½ cup dried sour cherries
1 cup chocolate milk
½ cup (1 stick) unsalted butter, melted
2 teaspoons vanilla
1½ cups all-purpose flour
1 cup ground sweet chocolate, divided
1 cup granulated sugar, divided
2½ teaspoons baking powder
½ teaspoon salt
1¼ cups vanilla cola
¼ cup dark rum
½ cup packed brown sugar
Vanilla ice cream (optional)

1. Coat inside of **CROCK-POT®** slow cooker with nonstick cooking spray. Bring cola and dried cherries to a boil in small saucepan. Remove from heat; let stand 30 minutes.

2. Combine chocolate milk, melted butter and vanilla in small bowl; stir to blend. Combine flour, ½ cup ground chocolate, ½ cup granulated sugar, baking powder and salt in medium bowl; stir to blend. Make a well in center of dry ingredients; add milk mixture and stir until smooth. Stir cherry mixture into batter. Pour into **CROCK-POT®** slow cooker.

3. Bring vanilla cola and rum to a boil in saucepan. Remove from heat. Add remaining ½ cup ground chocolate, remaining ½ cup granulated sugar and brown sugar; stir until smooth. Gently pour over batter. *Do not stir.* Cover; cook on HIGH 2½ hours or until cake is puffed and top layer is set. Turn off heat. Let stand, covered, 30 minutes. Serve warm with ice cream, if desired.

Chocolate-Stuffed Slow Cooker French Toast

Makes 6 servings

Butter, softened

6 slices (¾-inch-thick) day-old challah*

½ cup semisweet chocolate chips

6 eggs

3 cups half-and-half

⅔ cup granulated sugar

1 teaspoon vanilla

¼ teaspoon salt

Powdered sugar (optional)

Fresh fruit (optional)

*Challah is usually braided. If you use brioche or another rich egg bread, slice bread to fit baking dish.

1. Grease 2½-quart baking dish that fits inside of **CROCK-POT®** slow cooker with butter. Arrange 2 bread slices in bottom of dish. Sprinkle with ¼ cup chocolate chips. Add 2 more bread slices. Sprinkle with remaining ¼ cup chocolate chips. Top with remaining 2 bread slices.

2. Beat eggs in large bowl. Stir in half-and-half, granulated sugar, vanilla and salt. Pour egg mixture over bread layers. Press bread into liquid. Set aside 10 minutes or until liquid is absorbed. Cover dish with buttered foil, butter side down.

3. Pour 1 inch hot water into **CROCK-POT®** slow cooker. Add baking dish. Cover; cook on HIGH 3 hours or until toothpick inserted into center comes out clean. Remove dish and let stand 10 minutes. Top with powdered sugar, if desired. Serve with fruit, if desired.

Tip: Any oven-safe casserole or baking dish is safe to use in your **CROCK-POT®** slow cooker. Place directly inside the stoneware and follow the recipe directions.

S'mores Fondue

Makes about 4 cups

1 pound milk chocolate, chopped

2 jars (7 ounces *each*) marshmallow creme

⅔ cup half-and-half

2 teaspoons vanilla

1 cup mini marshmallows

Banana slices, apple slices, strawberries and graham crackers

1. Combine chocolate, marshmallow creme, half-and-half and vanilla in **CROCK-POT**® slow cooker. Cover; cook on LOW 1½ to 3 hours, stirring after 1 hour.

2. Sprinkle top of fondue with mini marshmallows. Serve with banana and apple slices, graham crackers and strawberries.

 Chocolate Orange Fondue

Makes 1½ cups

½ cup whipping cream
1½ tablespoons butter
6 ounces 60 to 70% bittersweet chocolate, coarsely chopped
⅓ cup orange liqueur
¾ teaspoon vanilla
Marshmallows, strawberries and pound cake cubes

1. Coat inside of **CROCK-POT**® slow cooker with nonstick cooking spray. Bring cream and butter to a boil in medium saucepan over medium heat. Remove from heat. Stir in chocolate, liqueur and vanilla until chocolate is melted. Place over medium-low heat; cook and stir 2 minutes until smooth.

2. Fill **CROCK-POT**® slow cooker with warm fondue. Serve with marshmallows, strawberries and pound cake.

Fudge and Cream Pudding Cake

Makes 8 to 10 servings

1 cup all-purpose flour
½ cup packed light brown sugar
5 tablespoons unsweetened cocoa powder, divided
2 teaspoons baking powder
½ teaspoon ground cinnamon
⅛ teaspoon salt
1 cup light cream
1 tablespoon vegetable oil
1 teaspoon vanilla
1½ cups hot water
½ cup packed dark brown sugar
Whipped cream (optional)

1. Coat inside of 5-quart **CROCK-POT®** slow cooker with nonstick cooking spray. Prepare foil handles by tearing off three 18×2-inch strips heavy foil (or use regular foil folded to double thickness). Crisscross foil strips in spoke design; place in **CROCK-POT®** slow cooker.

2. Combine flour, light brown sugar, 3 tablespoons cocoa, baking powder, cinnamon and salt in medium bowl. Add cream, oil and vanilla; stir to blend. Pour batter into **CROCK-POT®** slow cooker.

3. Combine hot water, dark brown sugar and remaining 2 tablespoons cocoa in medium bowl; stir well. Pour sauce over cake batter. *Do not stir.*

4. Cover; cook on HIGH 2 hours. Turn off heat. Let stand 10 minutes. Remove with foil handles to wire rack. Cut into wedges to serve. Serve with whipped cream, if desired.

Triple Chocolate Fantasy

Makes 36 pieces

2 pounds white almond bark, broken into pieces

1 bar (4 ounces) sweetened chocolate, broken into pieces*

1 package (12 ounces) semisweet chocolate chips

2 cups coarsely chopped pecans, toasted**

Use your favorite high-quality chocolate candy bar.

**To toast pecans, spread in single layer in heavy skillet. Cook and stir over medium heat 1 to 2 minutes or until nuts are lightly browned.*

1. Line mini muffin pan with paper baking cups. Place bark, sweetened chocolate and chocolate chips in **CROCK-POT**® slow cooker. Cover; cook on HIGH 1 hour. *Do not stir.*

2. Turn **CROCK-POT**® slow cooker to LOW. Cover; cook on LOW 1 hour, stirring every 15 minutes. Stir in nuts.

3. Drop mixture by tablespoonfuls into prepared baking cups; cool. Store in tightly covered container.

Peanut Fudge Pudding Cake

Makes 4 servings

1 cup all-purpose flour
1 cup sugar, divided
1½ teaspoons baking powder
⅔ cup milk
½ cup peanut butter
2 tablespoons vegetable oil
1 teaspoon vanilla
¼ cup unsweetened cocoa powder
1 cup boiling water
 Chopped peanuts (optional)
 Vanilla ice cream (optional)

1. Coat inside of 5-quart **CROCK-POT**® slow cooker with nonstick cooking spray. Combine flour, ½ cup sugar and baking powder in medium bowl. Stir in milk, peanut butter, oil and vanilla until well blended. Pour batter into **CROCK-POT**® slow cooker.

2. Combine remaining ½ cup sugar and cocoa in small bowl. Stir in boiling water. Pour into **CROCK-POT**® slow cooker. *Do not stir.*

3. Cover; cook on HIGH 1¼ to 1½ hours or until toothpick inserted into center comes out clean. Turn off heat. Let stand 10 minutes. Scoop into serving dishes. Serve warm with chopped peanuts and ice cream, if desired.

Tip: Because this recipe makes its own fudge topping, be sure to spoon some of it from the bottom of the **CROCK-POT**® slow cooker when serving, or invert the cake for a luscious chocolatey finish.

Cakes & Breads

Orange Poppy Seed Cake

Makes 8 servings

1½ cups biscuit baking mix
½ cup granulated sugar
2 tablespoons poppy seeds
½ cup sour cream
1 egg
2 tablespoons milk
2 teaspoons orange peel
1 teaspoon vanilla
   Orange Glaze (recipe follows, optional)

1. Coat inside of 4-quart **CROCK-POT**® slow cooker with nonstick cooking spray. Cut waxed paper circle to fit bottom of **CROCK-POT**® slow cooker (trace insert bottom and cut slightly smaller to fit). Spray lightly with nonstick cooking spray.

2. Whisk baking mix, granulated sugar and 2 tablespoons poppy seeds in medium bowl; set aside. Blend sour cream, egg, milk, orange peel and vanilla in separate medium bowl. Whisk dry ingredients into sour cream mixture until thoroughly blended.

3. Spoon batter into **CROCK-POT**® slow cooker; smooth top. Line lid with paper towels. Cover; cook on HIGH 1½ hours or until cake is no longer shiny and toothpick inserted into center comes out clean. Invert cake onto wire rack; peel off waxed paper. Cool completely. Prepare Orange Glaze, if desired.

Orange Glaze: Whisk ¼ cup orange juice into 2 cups powdered sugar in small bowl. Cut cake into wedges; place on wire rack with tray underneath to catch drips. Spread glaze over top and sides of each wedge. Sprinkle 2 teaspoons poppy seeds over wedges; let stand until glaze is set.

Orange-Cranberry Nut Bread

Makes 8 to 10 servings

- 2 cups all-purpose flour
- ½ cup chopped pecans
- 1 teaspoon baking powder
- ½ teaspoon baking soda
- ¼ teaspoon salt
- 1 cup dried cranberries
- 2 teaspoons dried orange peel
- ⅔ cup boiling water
- ¾ cup sugar
- 2 tablespoons shortening
- 1 egg, lightly beaten
- 1 teaspoon vanilla

1. Coat inside of round 3-quart **CROCK-POT®** slow cooker with nonstick cooking spray. Combine flour, pecans, baking powder, baking soda and salt in medium bowl; stir to blend.

2. Combine cranberries and orange peel in another medium bowl; stir in boiling water. Add sugar, shortening, egg and vanilla; stir just until blended. Add flour mixture; stir just until blended.

3. Pour batter into **CROCK-POT®** slow cooker. Cover; cook on HIGH 1¼ to 1½ hours or until edges begin to brown and toothpick inserted into center comes out clean.

4. Remove stoneware insert from **CROCK-POT®** slow cooker. Cool on wire rack 10 minutes. Remove bread from insert; cool completely on rack.

Tip: This recipe works best in round **CROCK-POT®** slow cookers.

Cinn-Sational Swirl Cake

Makes 10 to 12 servings

1 box (about 21 ounces) cinnamon swirl cake mix

1 cup sour cream

1 cup cinnamon-flavored baking chips

1 package (4-serving size) instant French vanilla pudding and pie filling mix

1 cup water

¾ cup vegetable oil

Cinnamon ice cream (optional)

1. Coat inside of 5-quart **CROCK-POT®** slow cooker with nonstick cooking spray. Prepare foil handles by tearing off three 18×2-inch strips heavy foil (or use regular foil folded to double thickness). Crisscross foil strips in spoke design; place in **CROCK-POT®** slow cooker.

2. Set cinnamon swirl mix packet aside. Sprinkle remaining cake mix into **CROCK-POT®** slow cooker.

3. Add sour cream, cinnamon chips, pudding mix, water and oil; stir to blend. Batter will be slightly lumpy. Add reserved cinnamon swirl mix, slowly swirling through batter with knife.

4. Cover; cook on LOW 3 to 4 hours or on HIGH 1½ to 1¾ hours or until toothpick inserted into center of cake comes out clean. Turn off heat. Let stand 10 minutes. Remove with foil handles. Serve warm with ice cream, if desired.

Bran Muffin Bread

Makes 1 loaf

¼ cup (½ stick) unsalted butter, melted, plus additional for mold

2 cups whole wheat flour, plus additional for dusting*

2 cups all-bran cereal

2 teaspoons baking powder

1 teaspoon baking soda

½ teaspoon salt

¼ teaspoon ground cinnamon

1 egg

1½ cups buttermilk

¼ cup molasses

1 cup chopped walnuts

½ cup raisins

Fresh fruit (optional)

Honey (optional)

*For proper texture of finished bread, spoon flour into measuring cup and level off. Do not dip into bag, pack down flour or tap on counter to level when measuring.

1. Butter and flour an 8-cup mold that fits inside of 6-quart **CROCK-POT®** slow cooker. Combine cereal, 2 cups flour, baking powder, baking soda, salt and cinnamon in large bowl; stir to blend.

2. Beat egg in medium bowl with electric mixer 1 minute. Add buttermilk, molasses and ¼ cup melted butter; beat well to blend. Add buttermilk mixture to flour mixture; stir just until combined. Stir in walnuts and raisins. Spoon batter into prepared mold. Cover with buttered foil, butter side down.

3. Place rack in **CROCK-POT®** slow cooker. Pour 1 inch hot water into **CROCK-POT®** slow cooker (water should not come to top of rack). Place mold on rack. Cover; cook on LOW 3½ to 4 hours or until bread pulls away from sides of mold and toothpick inserted into center comes out clean.

4. Remove mold from **CROCK-POT®** slow cooker. Let stand 10 minutes. Remove foil and run rubber spatula around outer edges, lifting bottom slightly to loosen. Invert bread onto wire rack. Let stand 10 minutes. Slice and serve with fruit and honey, if desired.

Glazed Cinnamon Coffee Cake

Makes 6 to 8 servings

1¾ cups biscuit baking mix, divided

¼ cup packed light brown sugar

½ teaspoon ground cinnamon

¾ cup granulated sugar

½ cup vanilla or plain yogurt

1 egg, lightly beaten

1 teaspoon vanilla

Glaze (recipe follows)

1. Coat inside of round 4-quart **CROCK-POT**® slow cooker with nonstick cooking spray. Prepare foil handles by tearing off three 18×2-inch strips heavy foil (or use regular foil folded to double thickness). Crisscross foil strips in spoke design; place in **CROCK-POT**® slow cooker.

2. Blend ¼ cup baking mix, brown sugar and cinnamon in small bowl; set aside.

3. Combine remaining 1½ cups baking mix, granulated sugar, yogurt, egg and vanilla in medium bowl; stir to blend. Spoon half of batter into **CROCK-POT**® slow cooker. Sprinkle half of cinnamon-sugar mixture over top. Repeat with remaining batter and cinnamon-sugar mixture.

4. Line lid with two paper towels. Cover tightly; cook on HIGH 1¾ to 2 hours or until toothpick inserted into center comes out clean. Turn off heat. Let stand 10 minutes. Prepare Glaze, if desired. Remove cake to large serving platter using foil handles.

Glaze: Whisk 1 to 2 tablespoons milk into 1 cup powdered sugar, 1 tablespoon at a time, until desired consistency is reached. Spoon glaze over top of cake. Cut into wedges.

Italian Cheesecake

Makes 16 servings

6 graham crackers, crushed to fine crumbs

2 tablespoons packed brown sugar

2 tablespoons unsalted butter, melted

2 packages (8 ounces each) cream cheese

1½ cups granulated sugar

1 container (15 ounces) ricotta cheese

2 cups sour cream

1 teaspoon vanilla

4 eggs

3 tablespoons all-purpose flour

3 tablespoons cornstarch

3 graham crackers, broken into 1-inch pieces (optional)

Fresh strawberries (optional)

Fresh mint (optional)

1. Coat inside of **CROCK-POT**® slow cooker with nonstick cooking spray. Prepare foil handles by tearing off three 18×2-inch strips heavy foil (or use regular foil folded to double thickness). Crisscross foil strips in spoke design; place in **CROCK-POT**® slow cooker.

2. Combine crushed graham crackers and brown sugar in medium bowl. Stir in melted butter until crumbs hold shape when pinched. Pat firmly into **CROCK-POT**® slow cooker. Refrigerate until needed.

3. Beat cream cheese and granulated sugar in large bowl with electric mixer at medium speed until smooth. Add ricotta, sour cream and vanilla; beat 3 to 5 minutes or until blended. Add eggs, one at a time, beating well after each addition. Beat in flour and cornstarch. Pour filling into prepared crust. Cover; cook on LOW 3 to 4 hours or until cheesecake is nearly set.

4. Turn off heat. Remove lid; cover top of stoneware with clean kitchen towel. Replace lid; cool 1 hour. Remove stoneware from base; cool completely. Remove cheesecake to large serving plate using foil handles. Cover; refrigerate until serving. Garnish with graham cracker pieces, strawberries and mint.

Orange Date Nut Bread

Makes 1 loaf

2 cups unbleached all-purpose flour, plus additional for dusting

½ cup chopped pecans

1 teaspoon baking powder

½ teaspoon baking soda

¼ teaspoon salt

1 cup chopped dates

2 teaspoons dried orange peel

⅔ cup boiling water

¾ cup sugar

1 egg, lightly beaten

2 tablespoons shortening

1 teaspoon vanilla

1. Spray inside of 1-quart soufflé dish with nonstick cooking spray; dust with flour.

2. Combine 2 cups flour, pecans, baking powder, baking soda and salt in medium bowl; stir to blend. Combine dates and orange peel in separate medium bowl; pour boiling water over date mixture. Add sugar, egg, shortening and vanilla; stir just until blended.

3. Add flour mixture to date mixture; stir just until blended. Pour batter into prepared dish; place in 5-quart **CROCK-POT®** slow cooker. Cover; cook on HIGH 2½ hours or until edges begin to brown.

4. Remove dish from **CROCK-POT®** slow cooker. Cool on wire rack 10 minutes. Remove bread from dish; cool completely.

Variation: Substitute 1 cup dried cranberries for dates.

Caramel and Apple Pound Cake

Makes 8 servings

4 medium baking apples, cored, peeled and cut into wedges

½ cup apple juice

½ pound caramels, unwrapped

¼ cup creamy peanut butter

1½ teaspoons vanilla

½ teaspoon ground cinnamon

⅛ teaspoon ground cardamon

1 prepared pound cake, sliced

Whipped topping (optional)

1. Coat inside of **CROCK-POT**® slow cooker with nonstick cooking spray. Layer apples, apple juice and caramels in **CROCK-POT**® slow cooker.

2. Combine peanut butter, vanilla, cinnamon and cardamom in small bowl; stir to blend. Drop by teaspoonfuls onto apples. Cover; cook on LOW 6 to 8 hours or on HIGH 3 to 4 hours.

3. Stir. Cover; cook on LOW 1 hour. Spoon apples over cake slices. Top with whipped cream, if desired.

Raisin-Oat Quick Bread

Makes 12 servings

1½ cups all-purpose flour, plus additional for dusting
⅔ cup old-fashioned oats
⅓ cup skim milk
4 teaspoons baking powder
1 teaspoon ground cinnamon
½ teaspoon salt
½ cup packed raisins
1 cup sugar
2 eggs, lightly beaten
½ cup (1 stick) unsalted butter, melted, plus additional for serving
1 teaspoon vanilla

1. Spray inside of ovenproof glass or ceramic loaf pan that fits inside of **CROCK-POT®** slow cooker with nonstick cooking spray; dust with flour.

2. Combine oats and milk in small bowl; let stand 10 minutes.

3. Meanwhile, combine 1½ cups flour, baking powder, cinnamon and salt in large bowl; stir in raisins. Whisk sugar, eggs, ½ cup melted butter and vanilla in separate medium bowl; stir in oat mixture. Pour sugar mixture into flour mixture; stir just until moistened. Pour into prepared pan. Place in **CROCK-POT®** slow cooker. Cover; cook on HIGH 2½ to 3 hours or until toothpick inserted into center comes out clean.

4. Remove pan from **CROCK-POT®** slow cooker; let cool in pan on wire rack 10 minutes. Remove bread from pan; let cool 3 minutes before slicing. Serve with additional butter, if desired.

Sticky Caramel Pumpkin Cake

Makes 8 servings

- 2 cups all-purpose flour
- 2 teaspoons baking powder
- 1 teaspoon baking soda
- ½ teaspoon salt
- ½ teaspoon pumpkin pie spice or ground cinnamon
- 1⅓ cups sugar
- 1 cup (2 sticks) unsalted butter, softened
- 4 eggs, at room temperature
- 1 can (15 ounces) solid-pack pumpkin
- 1 jar (16 ounces) caramel sauce or caramel ice cream topping

1. Trim sheet of waxed paper to fit bottom of **CROCK-POT**® slow cooker. Coat inside of 5-quart **CROCK-POT**® slow cooker and waxed paper with nonstick cooking spray.

2. Combine flour, baking powder, baking soda, salt and pumpkin pie spice in large bowl; stir to blend. Beat sugar and butter in separate large bowl with electric mixer at high speed 3 minutes or until blended. Add eggs, one at a time, beating well after each addition. Beat in pumpkin. Beat in flour mixture at low speed until smooth. Spread evenly in **CROCK-POT**® slow cooker.

3. Cover; cook on HIGH 2 to 2½ hours or until toothpick inserted into center of cake comes out clean. Place large plate upside-down on top of cake and invert the stoneware allowing cake to slide out onto plate. Peel waxed paper from bottom of cake, then invert onto large serving platter. Drizzle caramel sauce over cake.

Banana Nut Bread

Makes 1 loaf

⅓ cup butter

3 mashed bananas

⅔ cup sugar

2 eggs, beaten

2 tablespoons dark corn syrup

1¾ cups all-purpose flour

2 teaspoons baking powder

½ teaspoon salt

¼ teaspoon baking soda

½ cup chopped walnuts

Fresh strawberries (optional)

Sprigs fresh mint (optional)

1. Grease and flour inside of **CROCK-POT**® slow cooker. Beat butter in large bowl with electric mixer at medium speed 2 to 3 minutes or until fluffy. Gradually beat in bananas, sugar, eggs and corn syrup until smooth.

2. Combine flour, baking powder, salt and baking soda in small bowl; stir to blend. Beat flour mixture into banana mixture 3 to 5 minutes or until blended. Add walnuts; mix thoroughly. Pour batter into **CROCK-POT**® slow cooker.

3. Cover; cook on HIGH 2 to 3 hours. Cool completely; turn bread out onto large serving platter. Garnish with strawberries and mint.

Tip: Banana Nut Bread is a great way to use up those overripe bananas and the bread also freezes well for future use.

Fruity Favorites

Tequila-Poached Pears

Makes 4 servings

4 Anjou pears, peeled
2 cups water
1 can (11½ ounces) pear
    nectar
1 cup tequila
½ cup sugar
    Grated peel and juice
      of 1 lime

1. Place pears in **CROCK-POT®** slow cooker. Combine water, nectar, tequila, sugar, lime peel and lime juice in medium saucepan. Bring to a boil over medium-high heat, stirring frequently. Boil 1 minute; pour over pears.

2. Cover; cook on LOW 4 to 6 hours or on HIGH 2 to 3 hours or until pears are tender. Serve warm with poaching liquid.

Tip: Poaching fruit in a sugar, juice or alcohol syrup helps the fruit retain its shape and become more flavorful.

Bananas Foster

Makes 12 servings

12 bananas, cut into quarters

1 cup flaked coconut

1 cup dark corn syrup

⅔ cup butter, melted

¼ cup lemon juice

2 teaspoons grated lemon peel

2 teaspoons rum

1 teaspoon ground cinnamon

½ teaspoon salt

12 slices prepared pound cake

1 quart vanilla ice cream

1. Combine bananas and coconut in **CROCK-POT**® slow cooker. Combine corn syrup, butter, lemon juice, lemon peel, rum, cinnamon and salt in medium bowl; stir to blend. Pour over bananas.

2. Cover; cook on LOW 1 to 2 hours. To serve, arrange bananas on pound cake slices. Top with ice cream and warm sauce.

Apple-Date Crisp

Makes 6 servings

6 cups thinly sliced peeled apples (about 6 medium, preferably Golden Delicious)

⅓ cup chopped dates

2 teaspoons lemon juice

1⅓ cups uncooked quick oats

½ cup all-purpose flour

½ cup packed light brown sugar

½ teaspoon ground cinnamon

¼ teaspoon ground ginger

¼ teaspoon salt

Dash ground nutmeg

Dash ground cloves (optional)

4 tablespoons (½ stick) cold butter, cut into small pieces

1. Coat inside of **CROCK-POT®** slow cooker with nonstick cooking spray. Add apples, dates and lemon juice; toss to coat.

2. Combine oats, flour, brown sugar, cinnamon, ginger, salt, nutmeg and cloves, if desired, in medium bowl. Cut in butter with pastry blender or two knives until mixture resembles coarse crumbs. Sprinkle oat mixture over apples; smooth top. Cover; cook on LOW 4 hours or on HIGH 2 hours.

Tip: Simmer a sweet treat in your **CROCK-POT®** slow cooker during dinner, so you can delight your family and guests with a warm dessert.

Easy Peach Buckle

Makes 12 servings

2   packages (16 ounces
    each) frozen peach
    slices, thawed *or*
    5 cups fresh peach
    slices
¼   cup granulated sugar
1¾ cups all-purpose flour
½   cup packed brown sugar
2   teaspoons baking
    powder
1   teaspoon ground
    cinnamon
1   teaspoon baking soda
¼   teaspoon salt
1⅓ cups buttermilk
6   tablespoons canola oil
1   teaspoon vanilla

1. Coat inside of 5-quart
CROCK-POT® slow cooker with
nonstick cooking spray. Toss peaches
with granulated sugar in large bowl;
set aside.

2. Combine flour, brown sugar,
baking powder, cinnamon, baking
soda and salt in large bowl; stir to
blend. Combine buttermilk, oil and
vanilla in small bowl; stir to blend.
Stir buttermilk mixture into flour
mixture just until blended.

3. Spread batter evenly in
CROCK-POT® slow cooker. Arrange
peaches on batter. Cover; cook on
HIGH 2½ hours or until buckle
springs back when touched. Serve
warm.

Figs Poached in Red Wine

Makes 4 servings

2 cups dry red wine

1 cup packed brown sugar

12 dried Calimyrna or Mediterranean figs (about 6 ounces)

2 (3-inch) whole cinnamon sticks

1 teaspoon finely grated orange peel

4 tablespoons whipping cream (optional)

Orange peel strips (optional)

1. Combine wine, brown sugar, figs, cinnamon sticks and grated orange peel in **CROCK-POT®** slow cooker. Cover; cook on LOW 5 to 6 hours or on HIGH 4 to 5 hours.

2. Remove and discard cinnamon sticks. To serve, spoon figs and syrup into serving dish. Top with cream and orange peel strips, if desired.

Cherry Delight

Makes 8 to 10 servings

1 can (21 ounces) cherry pie filling

1 package (about 18 ounces) yellow cake mix

½ cup (1 stick) butter, melted

⅓ cup chopped walnuts

Place pie filling in **CROCK-POT®** slow cooker. Combine cake mix and butter in medium bowl; stir to blend. Spread evenly over pie filling. Sprinkle with walnuts. Cover; cook on LOW 3 to 4 hours or on HIGH 1½ to 2 hours.

Mixed Berry Cobbler

Makes 8 servings

1 package (16 ounces) frozen mixed berries

¾ cup granulated sugar

2 tablespoons quick-cooking tapioca

2 teaspoons grated lemon peel

1½ cups all-purpose flour

½ cup packed brown sugar

2¼ teaspoons baking powder

¼ teaspoon ground nutmeg

¾ cup milk

2 tablespoons unsalted butter, melted

Vanilla ice cream (optional)

1. Coat inside of **CROCK-POT**® slow cooker with nonstick cooking spray. Add berries, granulated sugar, tapioca and lemon peel; stir to blend.

2. Combine flour, brown sugar, baking powder and nutmeg in medium bowl. Add milk and butter; stir just until blended. Drop spoonfuls of dough on top of berry mixture. Cover; cook on LOW 4 hours. Turn off heat. Uncover; let stand 30 minutes. Serve with ice cream, if desired.

Tip: Cobblers are year-round favorites. Experiment with seasonal fruits, such as pears, plums, peaches, rhubarb, blueberries, raspberries, strawberries, blackberries and/or gooseberries.

Pumpkin Custard

1 cup solid-pack pumpkin

½ cup packed brown sugar

2 eggs, beaten

½ teaspoon ground ginger

½ teaspoon grated lemon peel

½ teaspoon ground cinnamon, plus additional for garnish

1 can (12 ounces) evaporated milk

1. Combine pumpkin, brown sugar, eggs, ginger, lemon peel and ½ teaspoon cinnamon in large bowl. Stir in evaporated milk. Divide mixture among six ramekins or custard cups. Cover each cup tightly with foil.

2. Place ramekins in **CROCK-POT®** slow cooker. Pour water into **CROCK-POT®** slow cooker to come about ½ inch from top of ramekins. Cover; cook on LOW 4 hours.

3. Use tongs or slotted spoon to remove ramekins from **CROCK-POT®** slow cooker. Sprinkle with additional ground cinnamon. Serve warm.

Variation: To make Pumpkin Custard in a single dish, pour custard into 1½-quart soufflé dish instead of ramekins. Cover with foil; place in **CROCK-POT®** slow cooker. Add water to come 1½ inches from top of the soufflé dish. Cover; cook as directed above.

Apple Crumble Pot

Makes 6 to 8 servings

4 Granny Smith apples
   (about 2 pounds),
   cored and *each* cut
   into 8 wedges

1 cup packed dark brown
   sugar, divided

½ cup dried cranberries

1 cup plus 2 tablespoons
   biscuit baking mix,
   divided

2 tablespoons butter,
   cubed

1½ teaspoons ground
   cinnamon, plus
   additional for topping

1 teaspoon vanilla

¼ teaspoon ground
   allspice

½ cup rolled oats

3 tablespoons cold butter,
   cubed

½ cup chopped pecans

   Whipped cream
   (optional)

1. Coat inside of **CROCK-POT**® slow cooker with nonstick cooking spray. Combine apples, ⅔ cup brown sugar, cranberries, 2 tablespoons baking mix, butter, 1½ teaspoons cinnamon, vanilla and allspice in **CROCK-POT**® slow cooker; toss gently to coat.

2. Combine 1 cup baking mix, oats and remaining ⅓ cup brown sugar in large bowl. Cut in 3 tablespoons cold butter with pastry blender or two knives until mixture resembles coarse crumbs. Sprinkle evenly over filling in **CROCK-POT**® slow cooker. Top with pecans. Cover; cook on HIGH 2¼ hours or until apples are tender. *Do not overcook.*

3. Turn off heat. Let stand, uncovered, 15 to 30 minutes. Top each serving with whipped cream sprinkled with additional cinnamon, if desired.

Poached Autumn Fruits with Vanilla-Citrus Broth

Makes 4 to 6 servings

2 **Granny Smith apples, peeled, cored and halved (reserve cores)**

2 **Bartlett pears, peeled, cored and halved (reserve cores)**

1 **orange, peeled and halved**

½ **cup dried cranberries**

⅓ **cup sugar**

5 **tablespoons honey**

1 **vanilla bean, split and seeded (reserve seeds)**

1 **whole cinnamon stick**

Vanilla ice cream (optional)

1. Place apple and pear cores in **CROCK-POT®** slow cooker. Squeeze juice from orange halves into **CROCK-POT®** slow cooker. Add orange halves, cranberries, sugar, honey, vanilla bean and seeds and cinnamon stick. Add apples and pears. Pour in enough water to cover fruit; stir gently to combine. Cover; cook on HIGH 2 hours or until fruit is tender.

2. Remove apple and pear halves to large cutting board; chop into 1-inch pieces. Strain cooking liquid. (Discard solids.) To serve, spoon fruit with sauce into bowls. Top with ice cream, if desired.

Tip: For a thicker sauce, return strained cooking liquid to **CROCK-POT®** slow cooker. Cook, uncovered, on HIGH 10 to 15 minutes or until thickened.

Peach Cobbler

Makes 4 to 6 servings

2 packages (16 ounces *each*) frozen peaches, thawed and drained

½ cup plus 1 tablespoon sugar, divided

2 teaspoons ground cinnamon, divided

½ teaspoon ground nutmeg

¾ cup all-purpose flour

6 tablespoons butter, cubed

1. Coat inside of **CROCK-POT®** slow cooker with nonstick cooking spray. Add peaches, ½ cup sugar, 1½ teaspoons cinnamon and nutmeg; stir to blend.

2. Combine flour, remaining 1 tablespoon sugar and remaining ½ teaspoon cinnamon in small bowl. Cut in butter with pastry blender or two knives until mixture resembles coarse crumbs. Sprinkle over peach mixture. Cover; cook on HIGH 2 hours.

Citrus Chinese Dates with Toasted Hazelnuts

Makes 4 servings

2 cups pitted dates

⅔ cup boiling water

½ cup sugar

Strips of peel from 1 lemon (yellow part only)

¼ cup hazelnuts, shelled and toasted*

Whipped cream (optional)

*To toast hazelnuts, spread in single layer in heavy skillet. Cook over medium heat 1 to 2 minutes or until nuts are lightly browned, stirring frequently.

1. Place dates in medium bowl; cover with water. Soak overnight to rehydrate. Drain; remove dates to **CROCK-POT**® slow cooker.

2. Add ⅔ cup boiling water, sugar and lemon peel to **CROCK-POT**® slow cooker. Cover; cook on HIGH 3 hours.

3. Remove and discard peel. Place dates in serving dishes. Sprinkle with hazelnuts. Top with whipped cream, if desired.

Fruit and Nut Baked Apples

Makes 4 servings

4 large baking apples, such as Rome Beauty or Jonathan
1 tablespoon lemon juice
⅓ cup chopped dried apricots
⅓ cup chopped walnuts or pecans
3 tablespoons packed brown sugar
½ teaspoon ground cinnamon
2 tablespoons unsalted butter, melted
½ cup water
  Caramel ice cream topping (optional)

1. Scoop out center of each apple, leaving 1½-inch-wide cavity about ½ inch from bottom. Peel top of apple down about 1 inch. Brush peeled edges evenly with lemon juice. Combine apricots, walnuts, brown sugar and cinnamon in small bowl; stir to blend. Add butter; mix well. Spoon mixture evenly into apple cavities.

2. Pour water in bottom of CROCK-POT® slow cooker. Place 2 apples in bottom of CROCK-POT® slow cooker. Arrange remaining 2 apples above but not directly on top of bottom apples. Cover; cook on LOW 3 to 4 hours or until apples are tender. Serve warm or at room temperature with caramel ice cream topping, if desired.

Rustic Peach-Oat Crumble

Makes about 8 servings

8 cups frozen sliced peaches, thawed and juice reserved

¾ cup packed brown sugar, divided

1½ tablespoons cornstarch

1 tablespoon lemon juice (optional)

1½ teaspoons vanilla

½ teaspoon almond extract

1 cup quick oats

¼ cup all-purpose flour

¼ cup granulated sugar

1 teaspoon ground cinnamon

¼ teaspoon salt

½ cup (1 stick) cold butter, cubed

1. Coat inside of 5-quart **CROCK-POT**® slow cooker with nonstick cooking spray. Combine peaches with juice, ½ cup brown sugar, cornstarch, lemon juice, if desired, vanilla and almond extract in large bowl; toss to coat. Place in **CROCK-POT**® slow cooker.

2. Combine oats, flour, remaining ¼ cup brown sugar, granulated sugar, cinnamon and salt in medium bowl. Cut in butter with pastry blender or two knives until mixture resembles coarse crumbs. Sprinkle over peaches. Cover; cook on HIGH 1½ hours or until bubbly at edge. Remove stoneware to wire rack; cool 20 minutes.

Cherry Flan

Makes 6 servings

5 eggs
½ cup sugar
½ teaspoon salt
¾ cup all-purpose flour
1 can (12 ounces) evaporated milk
1 teaspoon vanilla
1 bag (16 ounces) frozen pitted dark sweet cherries, thawed
  Whipped cream (optional)
  Fresh cherries (optional)
  Sprigs fresh mint (optional)

1. Coat inside of **CROCK-POT®** slow cooker with nonstick cooking spray. Beat eggs, sugar and salt in large bowl with electric mixer at high speed 3 to 5 minutes or until thick and pale yellow. Add flour; beat until smooth. Beat in evaporated milk and vanilla.

2. Pour batter into **CROCK-POT®** slow cooker. Place frozen cherries evenly over batter. Cover; cook on LOW 3½ to 4 hours or until flan is set. Serve warm with whipped cream, if desired. Garnish each serving with fresh cherries and mint.

Spiced Vanilla Applesauce

Makes 6 cups

5 pounds (about 10 medium) sweet apples (such as Fuji or Gala), peeled and cut into 1-inch pieces

½ cup water

2 teaspoons vanilla

1 teaspoon ground cinnamon

¼ teaspoon ground nutmeg

¼ teaspoon ground cloves

1. Combine apples, water, vanilla, cinnamon, nutmeg and cloves in **CROCK-POT**® slow cooker; stir to blend. Cover; cook on HIGH 3 to 4 hours or until apples are very tender.

2. Turn off heat. Mash mixture with potato masher to smooth out any large lumps. Let cool completely before serving.

Perfect
Puddings

Pineapple Rice Pudding

Makes 8 servings

1 can (20 ounces) crushed pineapple in juice, undrained

1 can (13½ ounces) unsweetened coconut milk

1 can (12 ounces) evaporated milk

¾ cup uncooked Arborio rice

2 eggs, lightly beaten

¼ cup granulated sugar

¼ cup packed brown sugar

½ teaspoon ground cinnamon

¼ teaspoon salt

¼ teaspoon ground nutmeg

Toasted coconut (optional)*

Pineapple slices (optional)

*To toast coconut, spread in single layer in small heavy-bottomed skillet. Cook and stir over medium heat 1 to 2 minutes or until lightly browned. Remove from skillet immediately.

1. Combine crushed pineapple with juice, coconut milk, evaporated milk, rice, eggs, granulated sugar, brown sugar, cinnamon, salt and nutmeg in **CROCK-POT®** slow cooker; stir to blend. Cover; cook on HIGH 3 to 4 hours or until thickened and rice is tender.

2. Stir to blend. Serve warm or chilled. Garnish with coconut and pineapple slices.

Pumpkin Bread Pudding

Makes 8 servings

2 cups whole milk

2 tablespoons butter

½ cup packed brown sugar

1 cup solid-pack pumpkin

3 eggs

1 tablespoon ground cinnamon

2 teaspoons vanilla

½ teaspoon ground nutmeg

¼ teaspoon salt

16 slices cinnamon raisin bread, torn into small pieces (8 cups *total*)

Bourbon Sauce (recipe follows, optional)

1. Coat inside of **CROCK-POT®** slow cooker with nonstick cooking spray. Combine milk and butter in medium microwavable bowl. Microwave on HIGH 2½ to 3 minutes or until very warm.

2. Whisk brown sugar, pumpkin, eggs, cinnamon, vanilla, nutmeg and salt in large bowl until well blended. Whisk in milk mixture until blended. Add bread cubes; toss to coat.

3. Remove bread mixture to **CROCK-POT®** slow cooker. Cover; cook on HIGH 2 hours or until knife inserted in center comes out clean. Turn off heat. Uncover; let stand 15 minutes. Prepare Bourbon Sauce, if desired; drizzle over pudding.

Bourbon Sauce: Combine ½ cup (1 stick) butter, ½ cup packed brown sugar and ½ cup cream in small saucepan; bring to a boil over high heat, stirring frequently. Remove from heat. Stir in 2 tablespoons bourbon.

Berry Bread Pudding

Makes 10 to 12 servings

6 cups bread, preferably
   sourdough, cut into
   ¾- to 1-inch cubes

1 cup raisins

½ cup slivered almonds,
   toasted*

6 eggs, beaten

1½ cups packed light brown
   sugar

1¾ cups milk

1½ teaspoons ground
   cinnamon

1 teaspoon vanilla

3 cups sliced fresh
   strawberries

2 cups fresh blueberries

Fresh mint leaves
   (optional)

*To toast almonds, spread in single
layer in heavy skillet. Cook over
medium heat 1 to 2 minutes or until
nuts are lightly browned, stirring
frequently.

1. Coat inside of **CROCK-POT**® slow cooker with nonstick cooking spray. Add bread, raisins and almonds; toss to combine.

2. Whisk eggs, brown sugar, milk, cinnamon and vanilla in medium bowl. Pour egg mixture over bread mixture; toss to blend. Cover; cook on LOW 4 to 4½ hours or on HIGH 3 hours.

3. Remove stoneware from **CROCK-POT**® slow cooker. Let bread pudding stand 10 minutes before serving. Serve with berries and garnish with mint leaves.

Plum Bread Pudding

Makes 12 to 16 servings

1 loaf (1 pound) sliced egg bread, lightly toasted*

2 tablespoons unsalted butter, divided

12 large unpeeled Italian plums, pitted and cut into wedges (about 4 cups *total*), divided

1½ cups plus 2 tablespoons sugar, divided

3 cups half-and-half

10 eggs

1¼ cups milk

2 teaspoons vanilla

¾ teaspoon salt

¾ teaspoon ground cinnamon

Sweetened whipped cream (optional)

Use an egg-rich bread, such as challah, for best results. For a more delicate bread pudding, substitute cinnamon rolls or plain Danish rolls.

1. Coat inside of 6-quart **CROCK-POT**® slow cooker with cooking spray. Cut toasted bread into 1-inch cubes; set aside.

2. Melt 1 tablespoon butter in large skillet over medium-high heat. Add half of sliced plums and 1 tablespoon sugar; cook 2 minutes or until plums are pulpy and release their juices. Pour plums and juices into medium bowl; repeat with remaining 1 tablespoon butter, remaining plums and 1 tablespoon sugar. Set aside.

3. Beat half-and-half, eggs, remaining 1½ cups sugar, milk, vanilla, salt and cinnamon in large bowl with electric mixer at medium speed 2 to 3 minutes until blended. Stir in bread, plums and any accumulated juices. Spoon into **CROCK-POT**® slow cooker.

4. Cover; cook on HIGH 3 hours or until pudding is firm when gently shaken and thin knife inserted halfway between center and edge comes out clean. Remove stoneware from base; cool 15 minutes. Serve with whipped cream, if desired.

Peach Bread Pudding:

If fresh plums are not available, substitute 9 large peaches, peeled, pitted and cut into wedges or 4 cups frozen sliced peaches, thawed (juices reserved).

Luscious Pecan Bread Pudding

Makes 6 servings

3 cups day-old French bread cubes

3 tablespoons chopped pecans, toasted*

2¼ cups milk

2 eggs, beaten

½ cup sugar

1 teaspoon vanilla

½ teaspoon ground cinnamon

Cherry Sauce (recipe follows, optional)

*To toast pecans, spread in single layer in heavy skillet. Cook over medium heat 1 to 2 minutes or until nuts are lightly browned, stirring frequently.

1. Prepare foil handles by tearing off three 18×2-inch strips of heavy foil (or use regular foil folded to double thickness). Crisscross foil strips in spoke design; place in **CROCK-POT®** slow cooker.

2. Toss bread cubes and pecans in soufflé dish that will fit inside of **CROCK-POT®** slow cooker. Combine milk, eggs, ½ cup sugar, vanilla and ½ teaspoon cinnamon in large bowl; pour over bread mixture in soufflé dish. Cover tightly with foil.

3. Place soufflé dish in **CROCK-POT®** slow cooker. Pour hot water into **CROCK-POT®** slow cooker to about 1½ inches from top of soufflé dish. Cover; cook on LOW 2 to 3 hours.

4. Lift soufflé dish from **CROCK-POT®** slow cooker using foil handles. Prepare Cherry Sauce, if desired; serve with bread pudding.

Cherry Sauce: Combine ¾ cup cranberry juice cocktail and ¼ teaspoon ground cinnamon in small saucepan; stir in 1½ cups cherries. Bring to a boil over medium heat; cook 5 minutes. Remove from heat. Stir in 2 tablespoons sugar until dissolved.

Coconut Rice Pudding

Makes 6 servings

2 cups water

1 cup uncooked converted long grain rice

1 tablespoon unsalted butter

Pinch salt

2¼ cups evaporated milk

1 can (14 ounces) cream of coconut

½ cup golden raisins

3 egg yolks, beaten

Grated peel of 2 limes

1 teaspoon vanilla

Toasted shredded coconut (optional)*

*To toast coconut, spread in single layer in heavy skillet. Cook over medium heat 1 to 2 minutes until lightly browned, stirring frequently. Remove from skillet immediately.

1. Place water, rice, butter and salt in medium saucepan. Bring to a boil over high heat, stirring frequently. Reduce heat to low. Cover; cook 10 to 12 minutes. Remove from heat. Let stand, covered, 5 minutes.

2. Meanwhile, coat inside of **CROCK-POT**® slow cooker with nonstick cooking spray. Add evaporated milk, cream of coconut, raisins, egg yolks, lime peel and vanilla; stir to blend. Add rice; stir until blended.

3. Cover; cook on LOW 4 hours or on HIGH 2 hours, stirring every 30 minutes. Pudding will thicken as it cools. Garnish each serving with shredded coconut.

English Bread Pudding

Makes 6 to 8 servings

16 slices day-old, firm-
textured white bread
(1 small loaf)

1¾ cups milk

1 package (8 ounces)
mixed dried fruit, cut
into small pieces

1 medium apple, chopped

½ cup chopped nuts

⅓ cup packed brown sugar

¼ cup (½ stick) butter,
melted

1 egg, lightly beaten

1 teaspoon ground
cinnamon

¼ teaspoon ground
nutmeg

¼ teaspoon ground cloves
Apple slices (optional)

1. Tear bread, with crusts, into 1- to 2-inch pieces; place in **CROCK-POT**® slow cooker. Pour milk over bread; let soak 30 minutes. Stir in dried fruit, chopped apples and nuts.

2. Combine brown sugar, butter, egg, cinnamon, nutmeg and cloves in small bowl; stir to blend. Pour over bread mixture in **CROCK-POT**® slow cooker; stir to blend. Cover; cook on LOW 3½ to 4 hours or until toothpick inserted into center comes out clean. Garnish with apple slices.

Note: To make chopping dried fruits easier, cut fruit with kitchen scissors or chef's knife sprayed with nonstick cooking spray.

Cran-Cherry Bread Pudding

Makes 12 servings

1½ cups light cream
3 egg yolks, beaten
⅓ cup sugar
¼ teaspoon kosher salt
1½ teaspoons cherry extract
⅔ cup dried sweetened cranberries
⅔ cup golden raisins
½ cup whole candied red cherries, halved
½ cup dry sherry
9 cups unseasoned stuffing mix
1 cup white chocolate baking chips
   Whipped cream (optional)

1. Coat inside of **CROCK-POT**® slow cooker with nonstick cooking spray. Prepare foil handles by tearing off three 18×2-inch strips heavy foil (or use regular foil folded to double thickness). Crisscross foil strips in spoke design; place in **CROCK-POT**® slow cooker.

2. Combine cream, egg yolks, sugar and salt in medium saucepan. Heat over medium heat until mixture coats back of spoon. Set saucepan in bowl of ice water; stir to cool. Stir in cherry extract. Remove to large bowl; press plastic wrap onto surface of custard. Refrigerate.

3. Combine cranberries, raisins and cherries in small bowl. Heat sherry in small saucepan until warm. Pour over fruit; let stand 10 minutes.

4. Fold stuffing mix and baking chips into custard. Drain fruit, reserving sherry; stir into custard. Pour into prepared dish. Top with reserved sherry; cover tightly with foil. Place on foil handles in **CROCK-POT**® slow cooker. Add water to come 1 inch up side of dish.

5. Cover; cook on LOW 3½ to 5½ hours or until pudding springs back when touched. Remove dish using foil handles. Uncover; let stand 10 minutes. Serve warm with whipped cream, if desired.

Apple-Pecan Bread Pudding

Makes 8 servings

8 cups bread, cubed

3 cups Granny Smith apples, cubed

1 cup chopped pecans

8 eggs

1 can (12 ounces) evaporated milk

1 cup packed brown sugar

½ cup apple cider or apple juice

2 teaspoons ground cinnamon

1 teaspoon ground nutmeg

1 teaspoon vanilla

½ teaspoon salt

½ teaspoon ground allspice

Ice cream (optional)

Caramel topping (optional)

1. Coat inside of **CROCK-POT®** slow cooker with nonstick cooking spray. Add bread cubes, apples and pecans.

2. Combine eggs, evaporated milk, brown sugar, apple cider, cinnamon, nutmeg, vanilla, salt and allspice in large bowl; stir to blend. Pour egg mixture into **CROCK-POT®** slow cooker. Cover; cook on LOW 3 hours. Serve with ice cream topped with caramel sauce, if desired.

French Toast Bread Pudding

Makes 6 to 8 servings

2 tablespoons packed dark brown sugar

2½ teaspoons ground cinnamon

1 loaf (24 ounces) Texas toast-style bread, *each slice cut in half diagonally**

2 cups whipping cream

2 cups half-and-half

2 teaspoons vanilla

¼ teaspoon salt

1¼ cups granulated sugar

4 egg yolks

¼ teaspoon ground nutmeg

Whipped cream (optional)

If unavailable, cut day-old 24-ounce loaf of white sandwich bread into 1-inch-thick slices.

1. Coat inside of **CROCK-POT**® slow cooker with nonstick cooking spray. Combine brown sugar and cinnamon in small bowl; stir to blend. Reserve 1 tablespoon; set aside.

2. Arrange bread slices in single layer in bottom of **CROCK-POT**® slow cooker. Sprinkle rounded tablespoon of cinnamon mixture over bread. Repeat layering with remaining bread and cinnamon mixture.

3. Combine whipping cream, half-and-half, vanilla and salt in large saucepan; cook and stir over medium heat. Reduce heat to low.

4. Whisk granulated sugar and egg yolks in medium bowl. Whisking constantly, add ¼ cup of hot cream mixture to egg mixture. Add egg mixture to saucepan. Increase heat to medium-high; cook and stir 5 minutes or until slightly thickened. *Do not boil.*

5. Remove cream mixture from heat; stir in nutmeg. Pour cream mixture over bread; press bread down lightly. Sprinkle reserved cinnamon mixture on top. Cover; cook on LOW 3 to 4 hours or on HIGH 1½ to 2 hours or until toothpick inserted into center comes out clean.

6. Turn off heat; uncover. Let pudding rest 10 minutes before spooning into bowls. Serve with whipped cream, if desired.

Sweet Sips

Triple Delicious Hot Chocolate

Makes 6 servings

3 cups milk, divided
⅓ cup sugar
¼ cup unsweetened cocoa powder
¼ teaspoon salt
¾ teaspoon vanilla
1 cup whipping cream
1 square (1 ounce) bittersweet chocolate, chopped
1 square (1 ounce) white chocolate, chopped
Whipped cream (optional)
Mini semisweet chocolate chips (optional)

1. Combine ½ cup milk, sugar, cocoa and salt in **CROCK-POT®** slow cooker; whisk until smooth. Stir in remaining 2½ cups milk and vanilla. Cover; cook on LOW 2 hours.

2. Stir in cream. Cover; cook on LOW 10 minutes. Stir in bittersweet and white chocolate until melted.

3. Pour hot chocolate into mugs. Top each serving with whipped cream and 1 teaspoon chocolate chips, if desired.

Hot Tropics Sipper

Makes 8 servings

4 cups pineapple juice

2 cups apple juice

1 container (about 11 ounces) apricot nectar

½ cup packed dark brown sugar

1 medium orange, thinly sliced, plus additional for garnish

1 medium lemon, thinly sliced, plus additional for garnish

3 whole cinnamon sticks

6 whole cloves

1. Combine pineapple juice, apple juice, nectar, brown sugar, orange slices, lemon slices, cinnamon sticks and cloves in **CROCK-POT**® slow cooker. Cover; cook on HIGH 3½ to 4 hours or until very fragrant.

2. Strain immediately (beverage will turn bitter if fruit and spices remain after cooking is complete). Remove and discard cinnamon sticks. Serve with additional fresh orange and lemon slices, if desired.

Mulled Cran-Apple Punch

Makes 8 servings

1 orange
1 lemon
1 lime
15 whole black peppercorns
10 whole cloves
10 whole allspice
3 whole cinnamon sticks, plus additional for garnish
1 (5-inch) square double-thickness cheesecloth
6 cups apple juice
3 cups cranberry juice
3 tablespoons maple syrup

1. Use vegetable peeler to remove 5 to 6 (2- to 3-inch-long) sections of orange, lemon and lime peel, being careful to avoid white pith. Squeeze juice from orange, set juice aside.

2. Place peels, peppercorns, cloves, allspice and 3 cinnamon sticks in center of cheesecloth. Bring corners together; tie with cotton string or strip of additional cheesecloth.

3. Pour apple juice, cranberry juice, maple syrup and reserved orange juice into 5-quart **CROCK-POT®** slow cooker; add spice bag. Cover; cook on LOW 5 to 6 hours or on HIGH 2½ to 3 hours. Remove and discard spice bag. Serve with additional cinnamon sticks.

Mucho Mocha Cocoa

Makes 9 servings

4 cups whole milk
4 cups half-and-half
1 cup chocolate syrup
⅓ cup instant coffee granules
2 tablespoons sugar
2 whole cinnamon sticks

1. Combine milk, half-and-half, chocolate syrup, coffee granules, sugar and cinnamon sticks in **CROCK-POT**® slow cooker; stir to blend. Cover; cook on LOW 3 hours.

2. Remove and discard cinnamon sticks. Serve warm in mugs.

Tip: If desired, add 1 ounce of rum or whiskey to each serving.

Ginger Pear Cider

Makes 8 to 10 servings

8   cups pear juice or cider
¾   cup lemon juice
¼   to ½ cup honey
10 whole cloves
2   whole cinnamon sticks,
    plus additional for
    garnish
8   slices fresh ginger

1. Combine pear juice, lemon juice, honey, cloves, 2 cinnamon sticks and ginger in 5-quart **CROCK-POT®** slow cooker.

2. Cover; cook on LOW 5 to 6 hours or on HIGH 2½ to 3 hours. Remove and discard cloves, cinnamon sticks and ginger before serving. Garnish with additional cinnamon sticks.

Warm Honey Lemonade

Makes 9 cups

4½ cups water
2½ cups lemon juice
1 cup orange juice
1 cup honey
¼ cup sugar
Lemon slices (optional)

1. Combine water, lemon juice, orange juice, honey and sugar in **CROCK-POT®** slow cooker; whisk well.

2. Cover; cook on LOW 2 hours. Whisk well before serving. Garnish with lemon slices.

 Chai Tea

Makes 8 to 10 servings

2 quarts (8 cups) water
8 bags black tea
¾ cup sugar*
8 slices fresh ginger
5 whole cinnamon sticks, plus additional for garnish
16 whole cloves
16 whole cardamom seeds, pods removed (optional)
1 cup milk

*Chai tea is typically sweet. For less-sweet tea, reduce sugar to ½ cup.

1. Combine water, tea bags, sugar, ginger, 5 cinnamon sticks, cloves and cardamom, if desired, in **CROCK-POT**® slow cooker; stir to blend. Cover; cook on HIGH 2 to 2½ hours.

2. Strain mixture; discard solids. (At this point, tea may be covered and refrigerated up to 3 days.) Stir in milk just before serving. Garnish with additional cinnamon sticks.

Viennese Coffee

Makes 4 servings

- 3 cups strong freshly brewed hot coffee
- 3 tablespoons chocolate syrup
- 1 teaspoon sugar
- ⅓ cup whipping cream, plus additional for topping
- ¼ cup crème de cacao or Irish cream

    Chocolate shavings (optional)

1. Combine coffee, chocolate syrup and sugar in **CROCK-POT®** slow cooker. Cover; cook on LOW 2 to 2½ hours.

2. Stir ⅓ cup whipping cream and crème de cacao into **CROCK-POT®** slow cooker. Cover; cook on LOW 30 minutes or until heated through. Ladle coffee into coffee mugs. Top with additional whipped cream and chocolate shavings, if desired.

Spiced Apple Tea

Makes 4 servings

3 bags cinnamon herbal tea
3 cups boiling water
2 cups unsweetened apple juice
6 whole cloves
1 whole cinnamon stick

1. Place tea bags in **CROCK-POT®** slow cooker. Pour boiling water over tea bags; cover and let steep 10 minutes. Remove and discard tea bags.

2. Add apple juice, cloves and cinnamon stick to **CROCK-POT®** slow cooker. Cover; cook on LOW 2 to 3 hours. Remove and discard cloves and cinnamon stick. Serve warm in mugs.

Warm and Spicy Fruit Punch

Makes about 14 servings

4 whole cinnamon sticks

1 orange

1 (8-inch) square double-thickness cheesecloth

1 teaspoon whole allspice

½ teaspoon whole cloves

7 cups water

1 can (12 ounces) frozen cran-raspberry juice concentrate, thawed

1 can (6 ounces) frozen lemonade concentrate, thawed

2 cans (5½ ounces *each*) apricot nectar

1. Break cinnamon sticks into pieces. Remove strips of orange peel with vegetable peeler or paring knife. Squeeze juice from orange; set juice aside.

2. Rinse cheesecloth; squeeze out water. Wrap cinnamon sticks, orange peel, allspice and cloves in cheesecloth. Tie bag securely with cotton string or strip of cheesecloth.

3. Combine reserved orange juice, water, juice concentrates and apricot nectar in **CROCK-POT**® slow cooker; add spice bag. Cover; cook on LOW 5 to 6 hours. Remove and discard spice bag before serving.

Tip: To keep punch warm during a party, place your **CROCK-POT**® slow cooker on the buffet table and turn the setting to LOW.

Mocha Supreme

2 quarts strong brewed coffee

½ cup instant hot chocolate beverage mix

1 whole cinnamon stick, broken in half

1 cup whipping cream

1 tablespoon powdered sugar

Whipped Cream Topping (recipe follows, optional)

Place coffee, hot chocolate mix and cinnamon stick halves in **CROCK-POT**® slow cooker; stir. Cover; cook on HIGH 2 to 2½ hours or until heated through. Remove and discard cinnamon stick halves. Ladle mocha mixture into mugs; top with Whipped Cream Topping, if desired.

Whipped Cream Topping:

Beat 1 cup whipping cream in medium bowl with electric mixer on high speed until soft peaks form.

Mulled Cranberry Tea

Makes 8 servings

2 tea bags
1 cup boiling water
1 bottle (48 ounces) cranberry juice
½ cup dried cranberries (optional)
⅓ cup sugar
1 lemon, cut into ¼-inch slices, plus additional for garnish
4 whole cinnamon sticks, plus additional for garnish
6 whole cloves

1. Place tea bags in **CROCK-POT®** slow cooker. Pour boiling water over tea bags; cover and let steep 5 minutes. Remove and discard tea bags.

2. Stir in cranberry juice, cranberries, if desired, sugar, 1 sliced lemon, 4 cinnamon sticks and cloves. Cover; cook on LOW 2 to 3 hours or on HIGH 1 to 2 hours.

3. Remove and discard cooked lemon slices, cinnamon sticks and cloves. Serve in warm mugs with additional cinnamon sticks and fresh lemon slices, if desired.

Hot Mulled Cider

Makes 16 servings

½ gallon apple cider

½ cup packed brown sugar

1½ teaspoons balsamic
   or cider vinegar
   (optional)

1 teaspoon vanilla

1 whole cinnamon stick

6 whole cloves

½ cup applejack or
   bourbon

1. Combine cider, brown sugar, vinegar, if desired, vanilla, cinnamon stick and cloves in **CROCK-POT®** slow cooker. Cover; cook on LOW 5 to 6 hours.

2. Remove and discard cinnamon stick and cloves. Stir in applejack just before serving. Serve warm in mugs.

A

Apple
Apple Crumble Pot, 66
Apple-Date Crisp, 56
Apple-Pecan Bread Pudding, 96
Caramel and Apple Pound Cake, 44
English Bread Pudding, 92
Fruit and Nut Baked Apples, 72
Hot Mulled Cider, 122
Hot Tropics Sipper, 102
Mulled Cran-Apple Punch, 104
Poached Autumn Fruits with Vanilla-Citrus Broth, 68
Spiced Apple Tea, 114
Spiced Vanilla Applesauce, 77
Apple Crumble Pot, 66
Apple-Date Crisp, 56
Apple-Pecan Bread Pudding, 96
Apricot
Fruit and Nut Baked Apples, 72
Hot Tropics Sipper, 102
Warm and Spicy Fruit Punch, 116

B

Baking Mix
Apple Crumble Pot, 66
Glazed Cinnamon Coffee Cake, 38
Orange Poppy Seed Cake, 31
Banana Nut Bread, 50
Bananas
Banana Nut Bread, 50
Bananas Foster, 54
Bananas Foster, 54
Berry
Apple Crumble Pot, 66
Berry Bread Pudding, 82
Cran-Cherry Bread Pudding, 94
Mixed Berry Cobbler, 62

Berry (continued)
Mulled Cran-Apple Punch, 104
Mulled Cranberry Tea, 120
Orange-Cranberry Nut Bread, 32
Warm and Spicy Fruit Punch, 116
Berry Bread Pudding, 82
Bittersweet Chocolate-Espresso Crème Brûlée, 16
Bran Muffin Bread, 36
Brownie Mix: Rocky Road Brownie Bottoms, 7

C

Cake Mix
Cherry Delight, 61
Cinn-Sational Swirl Cake, 34
Easy Chocolate Pudding Cake, 14
Cakes, 30–51
Easy Chocolate Pudding Cake, 14
Fudge and Cream Pudding Cake, 24
Hot Fudge Cake, 8
Peanut Fudge Pudding Cake, 28
Rum and Cherry Cola Fudge Spoon Cake, 18
Candy
Triple Chocolate Fantasy, 26
Triple White Chocolate Fantasy, 10
Caramel
Caramel and Apple Pound Cake, 44
Sticky Caramel Pumpkin Cake, 48
Caramel and Apple Pound Cake, 44
Cereal: Bran Muffin Bread, 36
Chai Tea, 111
Cherry
Cherry Delight, 61
Cherry Flan, 76
Cherry Rice Pudding, 88

Metric Conversion Chart

VOLUME MEASUREMENTS (dry)

$1/8$ teaspoon = 0.5 mL
$1/4$ teaspoon = 1 mL
$1/2$ teaspoon = 2 mL
$3/4$ teaspoon = 4 mL
1 teaspoon = 5 mL
1 tablespoon = 15 mL
2 tablespoons = 30 mL
$1/4$ cup = 60 mL
$1/3$ cup = 75 mL
$1/2$ cup = 125 mL
$2/3$ cup = 150 mL
$3/4$ cup = 175 mL
1 cup = 250 mL
2 cups = 1 pint = 500 mL
3 cups = 750 mL
4 cups = 1 quart = 1 L

VOLUME MEASUREMENTS (fluid)

1 fluid ounce (2 tablespoons) = 30 mL
4 fluid ounces ($1/2$ cup) = 125 mL
8 fluid ounces (1 cup) = 250 mL
12 fluid ounces ($1 1/2$ cups) = 375 mL
16 fluid ounces (2 cups) = 500 mL

WEIGHTS (mass)

$1/2$ ounce = 15 g
1 ounce = 30 g
3 ounces = 90 g
4 ounces = 120 g
8 ounces = 225 g
10 ounces = 285 g
12 ounces = 360 g
16 ounces = 1 pound = 450 g

DIMENSIONS

$1/16$ inch = 2 mm
$1/8$ inch = 3 mm
$1/4$ inch = 6 mm
$1/2$ inch = 1.5 cm
$3/4$ inch = 2 cm
1 inch = 2.5 cm

OVEN TEMPERATURES

250°F = 120°C
275°F = 140°C
300°F = 150°C
325°F = 160°C
350°F = 180°C
375°F = 190°C
400°F = 200°C
425°F = 220°C
450°F = 230°C

BAKING PAN SIZES

Utensil	Size in Inches/Quarts	Metric Volume	Size in Centimeters
Baking or Cake Pan (square or rectangular)	$8 \times 8 \times 2$	2 L	$20 \times 20 \times 5$
	$9 \times 9 \times 2$	2.5 L	$23 \times 23 \times 5$
	$12 \times 8 \times 2$	3 L	$30 \times 20 \times 5$
	$13 \times 9 \times 2$	3.5 L	$33 \times 23 \times 5$
Loaf Pan	$8 \times 4 \times 3$	1.5 L	$20 \times 10 \times 7$
	$9 \times 5 \times 3$	2 L	$23 \times 13 \times 7$
Round Layer Cake Pan	$8 \times 1 1/2$	1.2 L	20×4
	$9 \times 1 1/2$	1.5 L	23×4
Pie Plate	$8 \times 1 1/4$	750 mL	20×3
	$9 \times 1 1/4$	1 L	23×3
Baking Dish or Casserole	1 quart	1 L	—
	$1 1/2$ quart	1.5 L	—
	2 quart	2 L	—